Simply
SOCKS

Simply
SOCKS

45 Traditional Turkish Patterns to Knit

LARK BOOKS

A Division of Sterling Publishing Co., Inc.
New York

Editor: Leslie Dierks
Design: Dana Irwin
Photography: Evan Bracken
Illustrations: Charles Covington
Production: Elaine Thompson, Dana Irwin

Library of Congress Cataloging in Publication Data
Zilboorg, Anna, 1933–
   Simply Socks: 45 Traditional Patterns to Knit / Anna Zilboorg.
     p.   cm.
   Includes index.
   ISBN 1-887374-59-0
   1. Knitting--Turkey--Patterns.   2. Hosiery--Turkey.   I. Title.
   819.T9Z55   1994
   6.9'2--dc20   93-42128
                                     CIP

10 9 8 7 6 5 4 3

Published by Lark Books, a division of
Sterling Publishing Co., Inc.
387 Park Avenue South, New York, N.Y. 10016

Originally published in hard cover as Fancy Feet.
© 2000, by Anna Zilboorg

Distributed in Canada by Sterling Publishing,
c/o Canadian Manda Group, One Atlantic Ave., Suite 105
Toronto, Ontario, Canada M6K 3E7

Distributed in the U.K. by:
Guild of Master Craftsman Publications Ltd.
Castle Place, 166 High Street, Lewes East Sussex, England BN7 1XU
Tel: (+ 44) 1273 477374, Fax: (+ 44) 1273 478606,
Email: pubs@thegmcgroup.com, Web: www.gmcpublications.com

Distributed in Australia by Capricorn Link (Australia) Pty Ltd.
P.O. Box 704, Windsor, NSW 2756 Australia

If you have questions or comments about this book, please contact:
Lark Books
67 Broadway
Asheville, NC 28801
(828) 253-0467

Printed in China.

ISBN 1-887374-59-0

Dedication

To my Turkish sisters, who have given me more than I could have asked for, more than they could have imagined.

PHOTOGRAPH COURTESY OF REDHOUSE PRESS.

Acknowledgments

I want to thank Betül Tastan and Leyla Sürek of the Türkiye Is Bankasi for sending me a copy of Kenan Özbel's *Knitted Stockings from Turkish Villages*. It has been invaluable to me. I also want to thank Betsy Harrell for her enthusiastic encouragement, and Sherry Freeland, Mary Dashiell, and Arianne Dar for spurring me on to write this book.

In addition, for their indispensable assistance with studio and location photography, sincere thanks are extended to: Deborah Freed at Folklore in Asheville, North Carolina; Ishak (Ike) Korkmaz, the owner of Ike's International Deli in Asheville, North Carolina; Les Mitchell; French Sconyers-Snow; Sandra Soto at Native Expressions of Asheville, North Carolina; and Nancy and Tunç Togar, owners of Togar, Inc. of Arden, North Carolina. Thanks also to our models: Larry Bradshaw, Naeemah Hawthorne, Karla Holmes, Deborah Morgenthal, Corrina Morgenthal-Mathews, and Michelle Prince.

CONTENTS

Knitting in Turkey

TURKEY IS A LAND OF KNITTERS. In public parks, railroad waiting rooms, and buses, women are knitting. I once saw a woman sitting bolt upright on a concrete wall, knitting sweaters with eyelash yarn, while a man beside her was selling them to passersby. She was knitting in the English manner, since that is the appropriate method for eyelash yarn, but all the others were knitting continental style. No one I saw was knitting in the traditional Turkish manner. Westernization has taken over Turkish knitting, not only in the yarns used—they are now mostly acrylic—nor in the patterns—they are now mostly knit and purl designs—but even in the method of knitting itself.

IN TRADITIONAL TURKISH KNITTING, the yarn is tensioned around the neck and flicked with the thumb to make the stitches. The continental method may be more portable, but it is less accommodating for handling many colors at the same time, a practice that was common in the past. The traditional patterns, stranded in several colors, are fast disappearing in Turkey. The intent of this book is to save a few and publish them so that they may gain new life in other lands. They are marvelous patterns, worthy of emulation and of repetition.

ABOUT FORTY YEARS AGO, Professor Kenan Özbel of the Fine Arts Academy realized the increasingly precarious state of native handcraft and gathered a collection of Turkish knitting. His collection was exhibited in Istanbul, Ankara, Rome, Paris, and Finland. It was then divided and given to two museums—the Topkapı Palace Museum and the Bursa Archaeological Museum—to become part of their permanent collections. In recent years, under government orders, Professor Özbel's collection has been sealed in storage. Seeing it is forbidden. The curator of the museum in Bursa fears that their collection is rapidly rotting away in its cardboard boxes in the basement.

THERE ARE STILL A FEW OLDER WOMEN in rural villages who knit in the old style. I found some of their socks in the Antique Bazaar in Bursa, and those that I bought there are shown and charted amid the patterns in this book (see numbers 1, 13, 14, 16, 17, 37, and 44).

THESE SOCKS ARE MADE MOSTLY from wool, tightly worked. They are very stiff to the touch and feel as though they would wear forever. When I was in Erzerum, in eastern Turkey, and found myself unprepared for the cold, wet weather, I forced my feet into a pair of these somewhat forbidding socks. Within minutes I was toasty warm.

THE DEALER IN THE ANTIQUE BAZAAR said that he bought stockings from gypsies who traded with the villagers. Gypsies were familiar figures passing through village life, while he, on the other hand, was unable to trade himself since he was an outsider from the city. It seemed to me that it would be quite impossible for a foreigner without command of the Turkish language to make personal contact with the remaining traditional knitters. To begin with, travelers must deal exclusively with men. Village women, even more than urban women, are virtually invisible. Furthermore, there would be little chance of taking photographs, since devout Muslims do not allow their pictures to be taken. This is particularly true of Muslim women. In Doğubayazit, my companion wanted to take a picture of a street market where, among others, a fully veiled woman was shopping. A local man put his hand over the camera lens, angrily shook his head, and gestured toward the woman: her picture was not to be taken.

SOME VILLAGE WOMEN have moved to areas around Istanbul, and there, under the influence of the city and because of economic necessity, they have become more modern and sophisticated. One group from the province of Sivas, the home of some of the most complex Turkish knitting patterns, formed a cooperative of knitters during the 1960s. Both the cooperative and its products have been well documented by Betsy Harrell in her book, *Anatolian Knitting Designs* (Redhouse Press, Istanbul, 1981).

ON A RECENT TRIP TO TURKEY, Betsy Harrell revisited the co-op and found that the workmanship, already in decline earlier, had become worse and worse. This isn't surprising. The amount of work that goes into a well-made pair of socks is much greater than its commercial value, especially in the present-day market. The best of sock knitting will always be a labor of love.

History

LOOKING AT THE PRESENT STATE of knitting in Turkey, it is clear that the whole story of traditional Turkish knitting will never be known. The most basic questions—when and where it began—are themselves unanswerable. Surely it is an ancient tradition, perhaps as ancient as knitting itself.

KNITTING BEGAN IN the Middle East, sometime in the early centuries of the Common Era, and spread throughout the area, roughly following the spread of Islam. It is not unlikely that Turkish knitting was invented by seminomadic sheep herders, since it is an ideal craft for such peoples. Rug weaving was highly developed throughout the Middle East, and knitting, wherever it took hold, fed upon the more ancient craft. The wool yarn, the dyes, and the patterns are all directly linked to rug making. Over the centuries, many independent knitting patterns have developed, of course, but the familial likeness to rugs is quite apparent.

KNITTING IN THE BALTIC REGION also has a history that is lost in antiquity, and its designs are just as ornate as those of the Middle East in general and Turkey in particular. Knitting could have developed in the Baltic independently, of course, but there is evidence that suggests otherwise. First, the nature of the patterns is quite similar. Some Latvian mittens and Turkish socks look so much alike and so different from other knitting traditions that it is difficult not to look for links between them. Added to that is the braid stitch finish that decorates the edges of both

Northern mittens and Middle Eastern socks. As far as I know, this stitch exists nowhere else. A third similarity is the pointedness of mitten tips and sock toes.

ONE SOURCE OF CONNECTION between these two traditions might have been the North–South trade route from Byzantium through Russia that flourished from the ninth century until the Mongols overran ancient Russia in the thirteenth century. Knitting could have traveled along this route. I like to imagine an ancient Viking bringing home a knitted stocking, which was then carefully taken apart by Norse sheep herders and creatively reinvented.

Stockings in Turkey

WHENEVER AND HOWEVER knitting began in Turkey, by the time Kenan Özbel began his study, the art of stocking making had been deeply integrated into rural Turkish life. Especially in central Anatolia, sock knitting went far beyond practicality. The role it played in village life seems similar in some respects to that of quilt making in America. Girls learned to knit early in life and were expected to make socks for their trousseaux. Many stockings were given as gifts, particularly in conjunction with ritualized ceremonies such as weddings. An engaged girl would make special socks for her fiancé and would give socks to her new in-laws and to her wedding attendants. The bride also wore socks of different colors on each day of the wedding celebration. Each area had local patterns that were used for particular occasions. When a woman married outside her village, she would take her local patterns with her. Thus patterns spread throughout an area, gaining names

and changing names, melding with other patterns, and evolving into new ones.

I HAVE BEEN WRITING as though knitting patterns and styles were essentially the same throughout Turkey. This is by no means the case. In areas where mohair is the dominant yarn, socks are mostly white, with fine lace patterns. They are made fluffy by being placed inside a freshly baked loaf of bread. In the eastern, Kurdish parts of the country, the socks are loosely knit from undyed, unspun yarn, somewhat similar to Icelandic lopi. In some areas, embroidered stockings are the rule. The collection shown in this book contains one authentic Kurdish sock but is otherwise composed of multicolored stranded patterns of the type found throughout central Anatolia. While the others are lovely in their own right, the interplay of color in the Anatolian patterns offers particular interest for contemporary Western knitters.

THE YARN TRADITIONALLY USED to make these socks is unique. It is a strong, hairy, single-ply yarn that is coarse to the touch and knitted as tightly as possible—at 10 to 12 stitches per inch. The yarn looks as though it has been spun from the long guard hairs on the fleece and separated from the softer undercoat reserved for rug yarn. It makes sense that inferior wool would be utilized for less serious domestic purposes. The dyes used, however, are the same as those employed for making rugs, so the colors are strong and last the lifetime of the sock. Now commercial yarn, generally two-ply, is the norm. Sometimes (see sock 13), the leg is made of cotton and the foot of wool.

THE COLORS USED FOR STOCKINGS aren't limited to those found in rugs, or, at the least, they're used very differently in socks from the way they are in carpets. There are occasional splashes of shocking pink or bright turquoise in unlikely places. Sock 44 is a good example. (See the photo on page 14.) What could have motivated the bright pink in the heel? Possession of the yarn is the easy answer, but it is a choice I can't imagine an American or European knitter making. The fact that the pink is repeated at the top of the cuff indicates that the maker was aware of how it stood out and was trying to integrate it into the whole color scheme.

TURQUOISE IS PERHAPS more comprehensible, especially in children's socks, because it is felt to provide protection for the child. Many babies wear turquoise beads pinned onto their clothing or braided into their hair. Since quite a number of sock patterns have names such as "charms against the evil eye," it would be natural to knit them in turquoise.

KNITTING TECHNIQUES can be as unexpected as the colors. There is clearly a good deal of skill involved in working a complex pattern, particularly when a number of colors are used in each row. But there is remarkably little concern for the niceties of construction. For example, there appears to be no accepted way of beginning, except that all socks commence at the toe. Sometimes the toe is begun open, with a few stitches cast on circularly. The resulting hole might be sewn together, or it might be plugged with the ends of the yarn formed into a little tuft (see sock 16). Other knitters make perfectly smooth stitches across the toe.

AN EQUAL LACK OF CONSISTENCY or concern appears in the treatment of the heel stitches. They may even be cast on with a different color in a manner that leaves a sharp line across the back of the sock (see sock 44). In the West, knitters have developed many subtle ways of shaping, particularly when the goal is to make the heel fit comfortably; their counterparts in the East have been utterly uninterested in such things.

TURKISH KNITTERS are now making some attempt to shape heels in the Western manner in socks made for the tourist trade. This may be because buyers expect them to have that construction, perhaps because they fit better, or possibly because the Western style is simply assumed to be better. This shaping destroys the integrity of the patterning of the socks, and the ridiculous shapes that result from such attempts show that the knitters have no understanding of heel flaps and ankle shaping. With patterns they can do anything; with shaping they can do very little.

AS IN ANY FOLK TRADITION, the aesthetic sense of those who knit Turkish socks varies dramatically. There are women with fine artistic vision who have made objects of great beauty; there are some who simply imitate what they have seen; and there are those who are essentially uninterested in knitting and who do, at best, passable work. Since so much of the tradition has disappeared, and most of that which has been collected is unavailable, it would be folly to make any judgments except that the patterns are wonderful, and their possibilities endless.

Social Significance

IT WOULD BE EQUALLY FOOLISH to draw sociological or anthropological conclusions about the meanings and purposes of knitted stockings in Turkish village life. That socks are practical is obvious. That they have symbolic significance is also clear, but just what that significance might be is open not only to conjecture, but also to a variety of interpretations.

AT PRESENT the primary significance of these hand-knitted socks appears to be the small sum of money they fetch when sold. If it is true, as declared by the dealer in Bursa, that women don't knit because they prefer to watch television, one can hardly blame them. A pair of socks cost a pittance in the Antique Bazaar, and the price included two markups for two middlemen. Furthermore, because men are still largely in control of the commercial life of Turkey, it is quite possible that the women who knit the socks never see any of the money.

MEN ALSO PROVIDE most of the interpretation of the significance of the patterning and coloring on Turkish socks. Kenan Özbel declares authoritatively that patterns have quite detailed meanings; e.g., they signify that the wearer is orphaned, marriageable, married, or widowed.

ON THE OTHER HAND, when Betsy Harrell interviewed knitters from Sivas in Istanbul, she was told that patterns didn't mean anything (but a widow mustn't wear new socks in public). She also found the naming of patterns to be a casual matter. People didn't seem to care about names one way or another. While Professor Özbel considers pattern names significant, his book supports this casualness by example: the same pattern appears in different places with different names. Hence it seems most unlikely that the naming of patterns had any magical or sociological significance.

THE SEARCH FOR SIGNIFICANT MEANING may itself be sociological. A man in Üğrüp who had grown up in a village in Sivas province assured me that everything in the socks had meaning. He said that the socks were a way for adolescent boys and girls of the village to talk to each other. Outside their families, they had no social contacts with the opposite sex, and the boys only saw the girls—fully veiled—when they came to get water on Saturdays. That was when their socks would tell stories: the color yellow meant "I am dying of love." This man in Üğrüp was a romantic and a teller of tales. Although I wouldn't take his stories as fact, I can well imagine young boys questioning their sisters about other girls and all manner of games being played between them.

LIFE IN THE VILLAGES has been changing rapidly in modern times. The long tradition of hand-knitted socks has lost its meaning in village life and hence is disappearing. But even as it comes to an end in Turkey, this tradition has created a rich legacy of patterns to delight modern knitters everywhere.

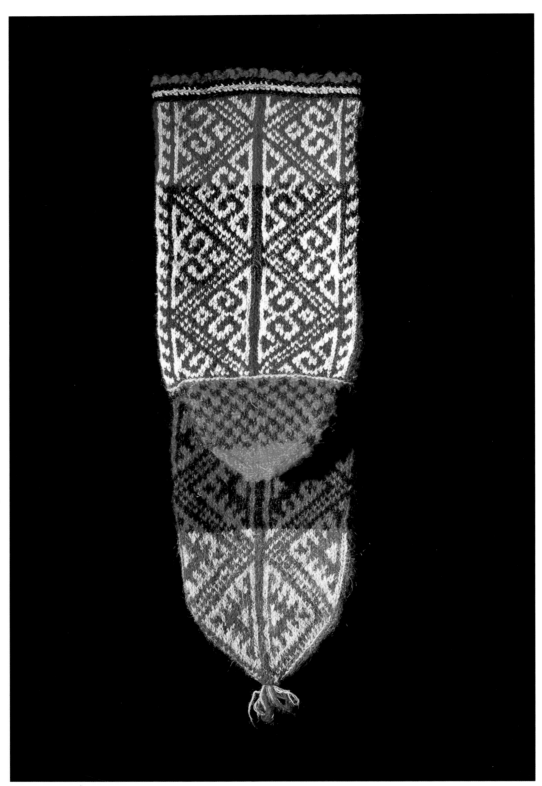

Splashes of shocking pink decorate sock 44 in unexpected places—at the heel and at the top of the cuff.

The Patterns and the Socks

TURKISH PATTERNS look quite different from Western ones, even when they are in fact similar. For example, some stars and triangles are the same all over the world, but these and other familiar patterns tend to appear unusual in a Turkish context. I think the difference arises from an Eastern principle of design that considers figure and ground to have equal importance. In the West we have no word for it, but it is similar to the Japanese vision of *Notan.* This results in a balanced pattern, where the eye often switches unconsciously between figure and ground. When a figure is used in a Turkish design, it is placed so that the ground makes another pattern. We see this in some Scandinavian knitting when star patterns,

touching points, create a background of diamonds and squares. For the most part, Scandinavian knitting avoids such an effect and instead places its stars so that they stand out against an amorphous ground.

TURKISH KNITTING tends to do just the opposite. It is surprising how many times

you can begin a Turkish pattern with a clear sense of what the design looks like, only to find a different pattern appearing as the knitting progresses. The color that you thought would make the design now becomes the background. Choice of color is an important factor in this process, but I have found that even with a cool ground color and a warm pattern color, my figure and ground can reverse.

ONE REASON the patterns are so likely to reverse is that they tend to have almost the same number of stitches in both figure and ground. Thus one useful way of making one shape stand out against another is to add more background stitches between pattern repeats. Another is to make the ground striped rather than solid in color. Striped grounds are frequently found in Turkish socks, and the stripes often change color to correspond with pattern repeats.

IN ADDITION TO the visual effects created, the balance of figure and ground makes the Turkish patterns surprisingly easy to knit. You are, essentially, knitting one pattern in one color and another in a different color. You build one up as you work the other down. This provides a rhythm and logic that your hands grasp even quicker than your mind can

15

understand. Usually my hands can learn a pattern well enough in one repeat so that I don't have to follow a chart the second time through; a glance now and then is enough. (It is true, though, that I copy every pattern before I work it. Making my own x's row by row on graph paper gives me a familiarity with the pattern before I begin.) Confusion is most apt to set in when the figure and ground are identical or nearly so, which is the case in a fair number of patterns.

QUITE A NUMBER of patterns are made up of only two or three different rows (see socks 29 and 30). How you begin each round determines the pattern. Also, many different patterns develop from a handful of small units. These are characteristics that become apparent as you work, making Turkish patterns, above all, fun to knit.

MANY OF THE PATTERNS have been refined over generations of use by people who are neither reading directions nor poring over charts. Instead, these women are following rhythms familiar to their fingers and keeping an eye on what they are doing. Since they knit in the round, the right side is always before them, so mistakes are easier to catch. And many mistakes become the beginnings of new patterns.

TURKISH PATTERNS tend to have more curves in them than Western designs, though many of the patterns are angular. The patterns are usually symmetrical vertically, but the symmetry that we would expect to find on the horizontal axis is often altered sightly (see sock 6). The number of stitches in each pattern repeat varies widely—from two to about 30.

Most of the patterns, however, have 14 or 16 stitches if they are medium in size and 22 or 24 if they are larger.

IN SOCKS, a large diamond pattern often marches down the front and back, and the accompanying half-diamonds on either side are usually done in a somewhat different design (see the foot of sock 37). To chart a complete pattern—for a sweater or vest—using this motif, you can either maintain the difference or use the pattern of the primary diamond exclusively.

TURKISH PATTERNS can be used effectively not only in socks but anywhere and everywhere. I agree with a professor of mine who once remarked that we don't honor tradition by slavishly imitating it. We can honor and give new life to this fine knitting tradition by using its patterns in a broader context. Many of the patterns won't work easily on punch card knitting machines because of the number of stitches in each repeat, but they are easy to do on an electronic machine. In hand knitting, they are applicable everywhere.

PATTERNS THAT APPEAR vertically on socks can easily be worked horizontally as borders. Small patterns can be made into stripes, and large patterns can cover a whole sweater, coat, or vest. They can also be used very nicely for mittens, with the sole pattern on the palm.

TO MAKE MITTENS from the patterns given here, it is best to start at the tip of the hand, following the directions for the Turkish toe. This makes an exceptionally smooth mitten tip, with a band of solid color that goes all around the mitten,

The pointed toe and triangular heel distinguish a traditional
Turkish stocking from its Western counterpart.

from one side of the wrist to the other. After increasing the tip, continue down the hand until you reach the place for the thumb. Make the thumb separately, insert it, leaving stitches on the palm and thumb to be grafted together later, and continue to the wrist. I find this a satisfying way of making mittens, especially since I would rather do the thumb separately than with the rest of the mitten hanging down alongside it.

FINALLY, OF COURSE, you can use Turkish patterns to make modern Western socks. Westerners tend to ignore feet and their aesthetic potential, but this is a pity. Turkish socks make feet look wonderful as well as feel good. They can easily travel under boots in winter and be worn without shoes in houses. (They will last longer and need washing less frequently if they're worn over a thin pair of plain socks.) When patterned in glitter, they make excellent party socks, and as house slippers, they're a natural.

THE ONLY DIFFICULTY is reinforcing the sole without undermining the aesthetics. One method is to use a tube of silicone from the hardware store, placing dots on the sole along the lines of the pattern. They will dry quite clear and provide a strong, nonslip base. The major drawback of this method is that the bumps can be felt while walking. The method I like best is to wear the socks until you can see exactly where they're going to wear through. Then patch this spot with a piece of leather. (Old gloves with split fingers are good sources for patches. In lieu of these, you can use leather patches made for elbows.)

THE MOST AMBITIOUS SOCKS to make are cross-country ski socks. For these you will want more stitches at the top than at the ankle. The side stripes on Turkish socks provide an excellent place to increase stitches up the leg (or decrease them down the leg) without disturbing the pattern.

ALL SOCKS WITH TURKISH PATTERNS can be knit from the top down if that is your preference. This has one advantage over the toe-to-top direction: the stitches you pick up for the heel are underneath the foot, so any irregularity in the pattern is less visible than it would be at the back of the leg. It is better, even working from the top down, to use an inserted heel for Turkish patterned socks. They may be a bit harder to get your foot into than the English heel, but they look much better.

THE SOCKS THAT FOLLOW have been knitted many different ways with different toes and different tops. The authentic ones from Turkey have all, except sock 37, been knitted from toe to top. Mine vary according to my inclinations while making them. I wanted to stress, by action as well as by words, that you can use any method you choose. The directions that follow, however, are for socks that go from toe to top, since that is the traditional Turkish way and the method least common in the West.

Generic Directions for Knitting Turkish Socks

BEGIN BY CHOOSING needles and yarn that will give about 6 sts/inch (24 sts/10 cm). You will need a set of five dp needles—preferably short—and, optionally, an 11-1/2-inch (29-cm) circular needle.

Select a pattern that will have 25–29 sts across the instep for an adult or 19–23 sts for a child, and draw several repeats of the pattern on graph paper. If you need to fill in extra stitches, add a filler pattern. Then decide where you want the pattern to end at the toe, drawing a line under the middle five stitches. Now draw up one square and out one square, increasing one stitch each side until you have the total number of stitches in the pattern. See the chart on page 21 for an example. When you've finished with the front, chart your sole the same way. You can use the same pattern for the instep and sole if you like, but it makes the heel more difficult.

CAST ON TOE: Holding two dp needles parallel, wrap the yarn in a figure eight around the needles until there are four loops on each needle (see Figure 1). Hold the tail down with your left thumb—or your right thumb if you're left-handed. Using a third

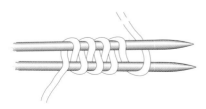

Figure 1

needle, knit the loops off the top needle without letting the loops on the bottom needle slide off (see Figure 2). Turn. With

Figure 2

another needle, knit the loops off the bottom needle. You will have to knit these through the back of the loop to keep them from being twisted. You now have a small piece of knitting with stitches on either end. Knit each row of stitches one more time. Your piece is now a small rectangle.

BEGIN TO KNIT AROUND: Pick up 3 sts on the side of the rectangle using a third nee-

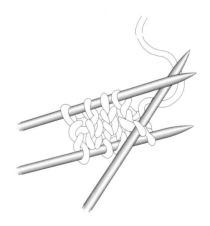

Figure 3

19

dle (see Figure 3). With another needle, work the 4 sts on the needle. Using another needle, pick up 3 sts on the other side of the rectangle. Again with another needle, work across the 4 sts on the remaining needle. You now have a square of stitches on four needles. On the next round, begin to follow your charts. Pick up 1 st at beginning and end of each pattern row. (Pick it up by inserting your needle into the previous row of the plain band. Keep 4 sts on each end needle. When you have increased all the stitches you need, work the end needle on the following round as follows: k2 tog, ssk. (This eliminates the stitches behind which you were increasing. It will leave a two-stitch band around your sock.)

WORK FOOT: Redistribute stitches on needles as desired, or switch to an 11-1/2-inch (29-cm) circular needle. Work up foot until 1-3/4 inches (4.4 cm) short of desired foot length. You can try it on as you go.

Put sole stitches on holder. Cast on, by the simple half-hitch method, an equal number of stitches for the back of the leg. Cast them on in both colors, following the chart for the next row of the pattern.

Work up the leg, following the chart on both front and back with the two-stitch band between. When you've gone as far as you want, finish the top in any way you choose.

FOR THE TRADITIONAL BRAID STITCH: Work 1 rnd, alternating colors, 1 st A and 1 st B. Sl 1 st from left needle. Bring yarn to the front. Return slipped st to left needle (to prevent a hole). Turn work so that the purl side is facing you. Knit 1 st B. *K1 A, bringing yarn *over* B; k1 B, bringing yarn *over* A. Repeat from * around (see Figure 4). The yarns will twist with each stitch, and you'll find it helpful to pull out a yard or two of each color before beginning.

When you reach the beginning of the round, work another round—continuing to alternate colors with each stitch—but this time bring the yarn for each stitch *under* the other. This will unwind the twisted yarn.

When the second round is complete, sl 1 st. Bring both yarns to front, and replace sl st. Turn work. Now bind off, alternating A and B, around the sock.

MAKE THE HEEL: Move the stitches from the holder onto two dp needles. Pick up cast-on stitches, following the *next* row of the pattern in the *opposite* direction.

If the pattern is at all complex, it is useful to draw the heel on your chart. To do this, mark the cast-on row. At the sides, mark two rows straight. Then decrease 1 st at each side of every row until 4 sts remain. This is a chart for half your heel. You will be decreasing a total of 4 sts every row.

Work around, following sole pattern on sole and freshly drawn heel pattern on the

Figure 4

20

back. Pick up 1 or 2 sts at each side to prevent holes. Work another round on which you decrease these extra stitches.

You should now have a back heel, a sole, and a two-stitch band on each side. Work around, following the patterns, decreasing at the beginning and end of the back and sole. Decrease so that the band eats up the pattern: at the beginning, ssk (left-slanting decrease) using band st and pattern st; at the end, k2 tog (right-slanting decrease) using band st and pattern st.

When you reach the end of your chart and have 12 sts left, break off the yarns. After arranging the stitches on two needles so that the bands face each other, graft the stitches together. Bring the ends of the grafting yarn to the inside, and give them a pull. The heel will shape up properly.

There is one piece of good news after all this fussy knitting: To be authentically Turkish, you need not weave in all the ends. Just cut them off, and let them hang.

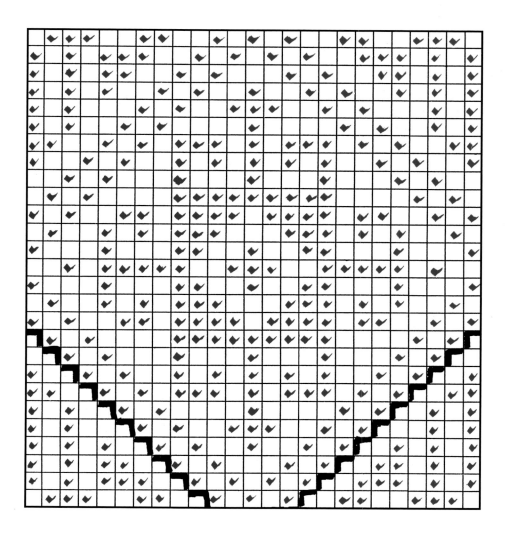

1

An authentic Turkish sock worked in 3 colors per row throughout
Secondary pattern at top: 15 stitch, 9 row repeat
Main pattern: 24 stitch, 17 row repeat

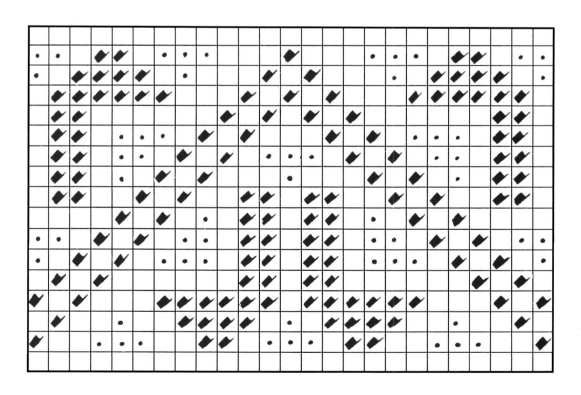

2

8 stitch, 14 row repeat

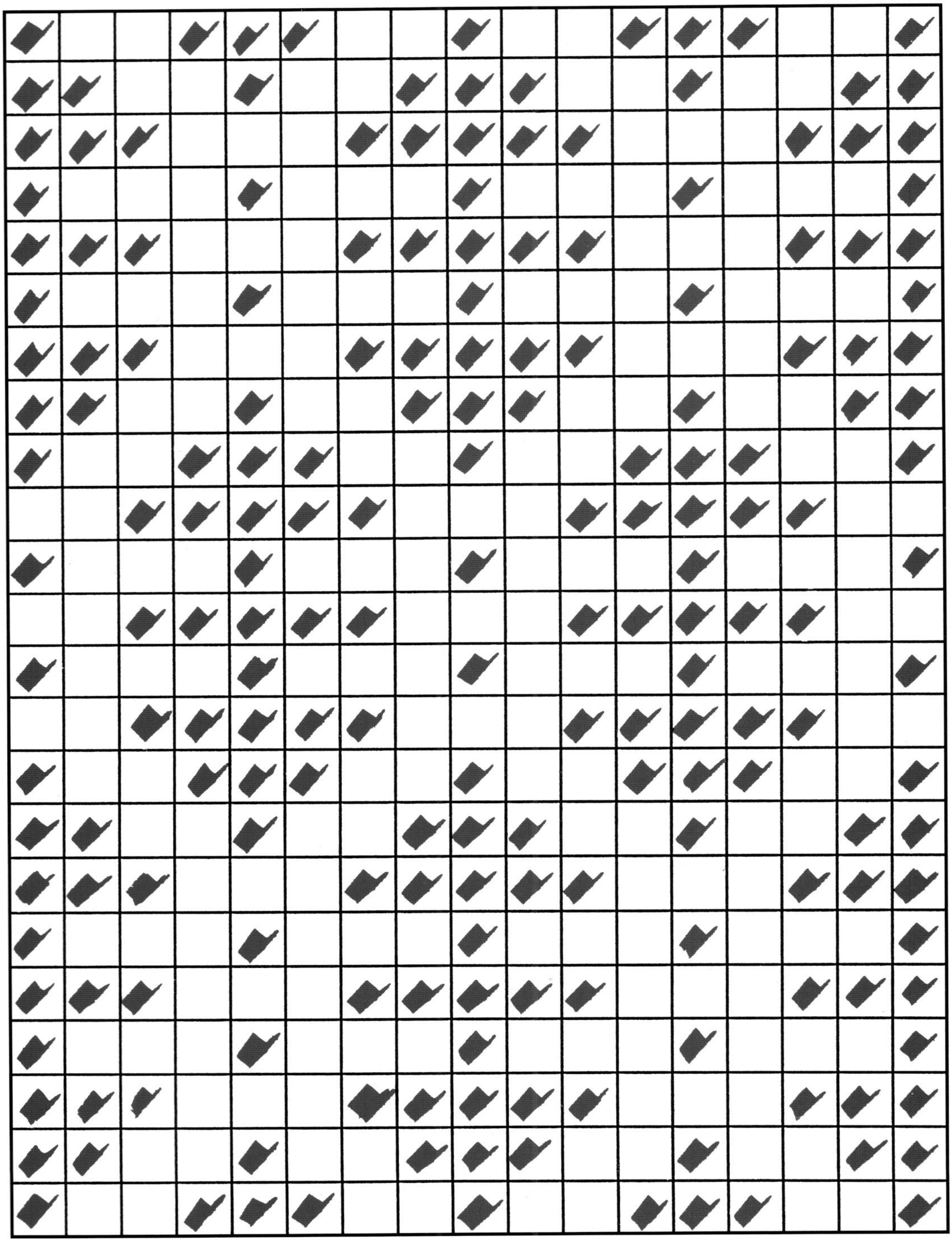

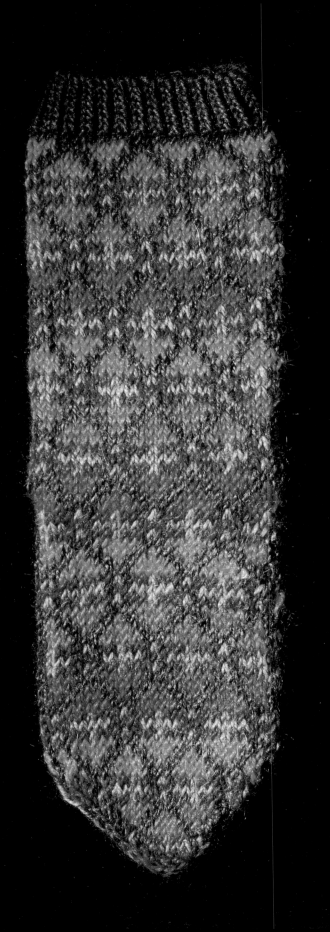

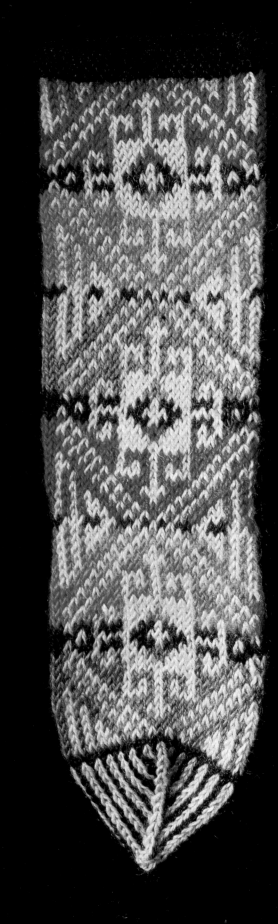

"Mirrors"
25 stitch, 26 row repeat

4

"Hand to Hand"
22 stitch, 26 row repeat

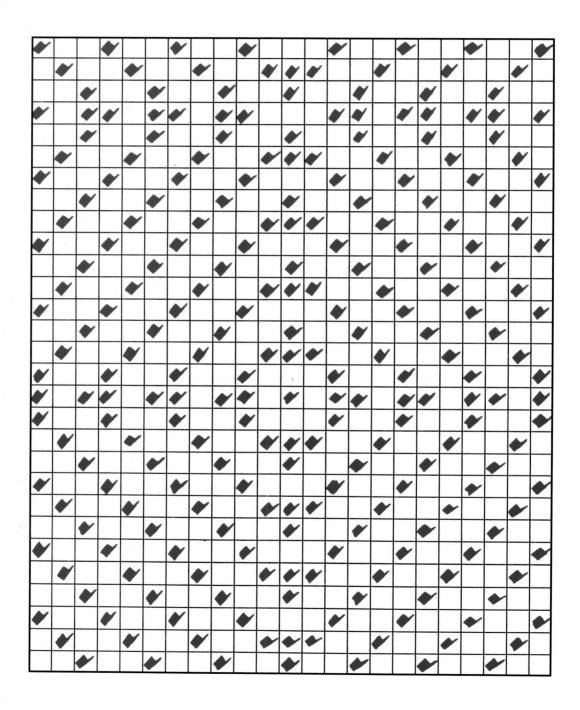

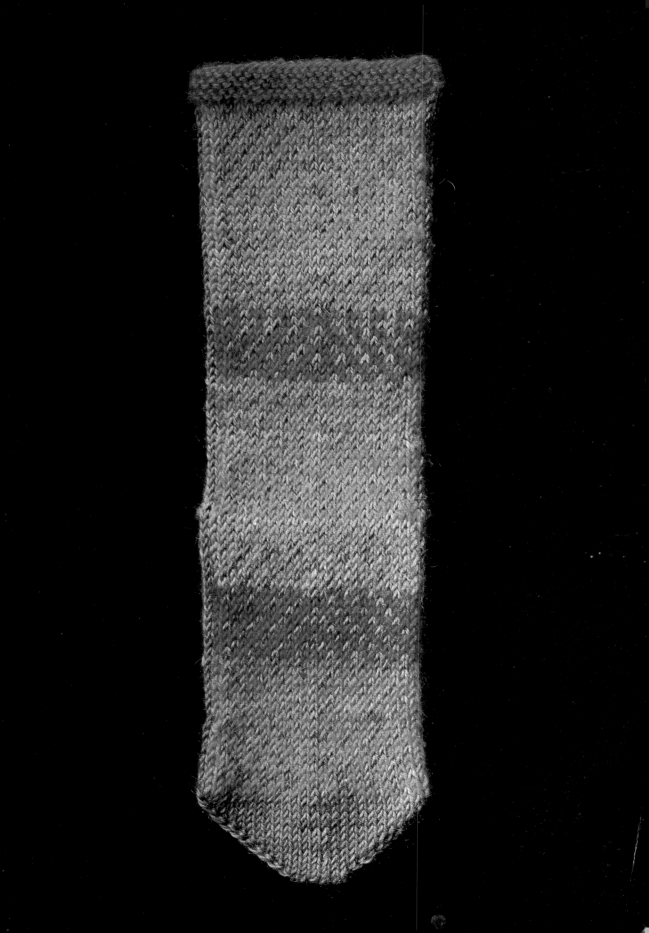

5

"Letter-bearer": 8 stitch, 5 row repeat
"Dogs": 20 stitch, 8 row repeat

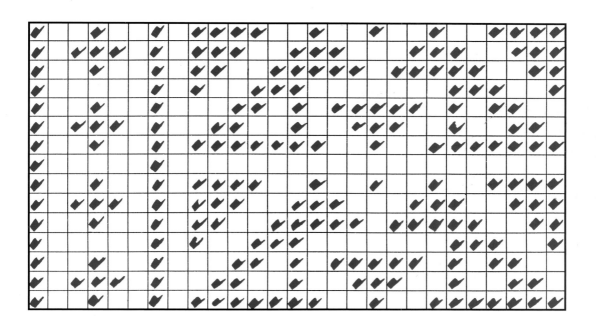

6

"Elbistan": 27 stitch, 24 row repeat
(The pattern outside the diamond often appears alone and is called an apple.
Although it looks very different, it's just a small variation on the Elbistan stitch.)

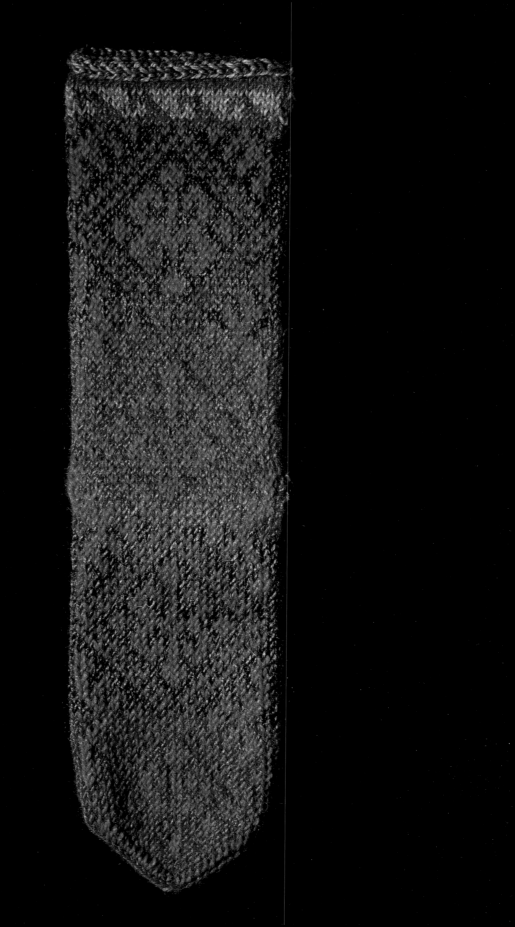

"Hook": 6 stitch, 8 row repeat
"Earring": 6 stitch, 16 row repeat

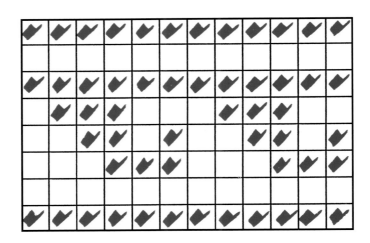

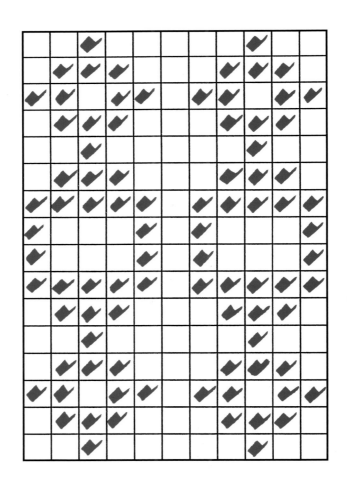

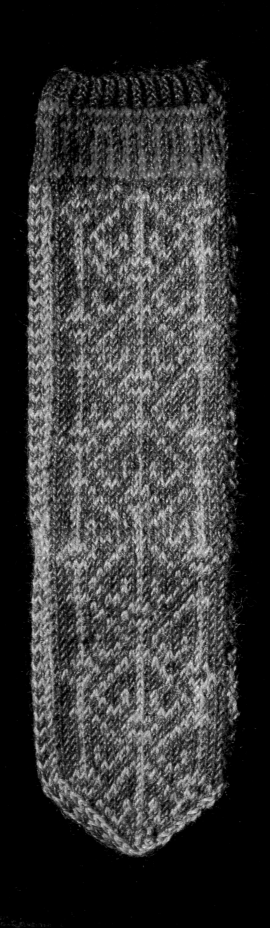

8

Secondary pattern at top: 4 stitch, 7 row repeat
"Cranes": 16 stitch, 14 row repeat

A child's sweater knitted in the "cranes" pattern.

The mother's sweater is knitted in the "boxes" pattern, and her child's sweater is made in a pattern very similar to "triangles."

9

Main pattern: 9 stitch, 9 row repeat
Secondary pattern: 4 stitch, 3 row repeat

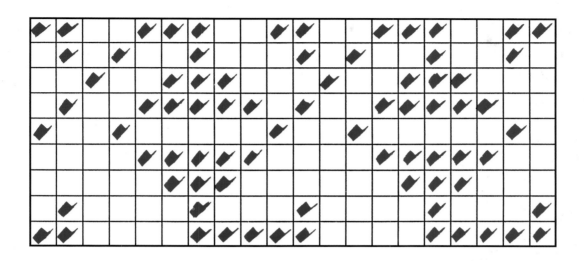

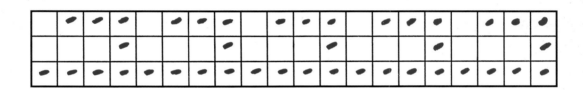

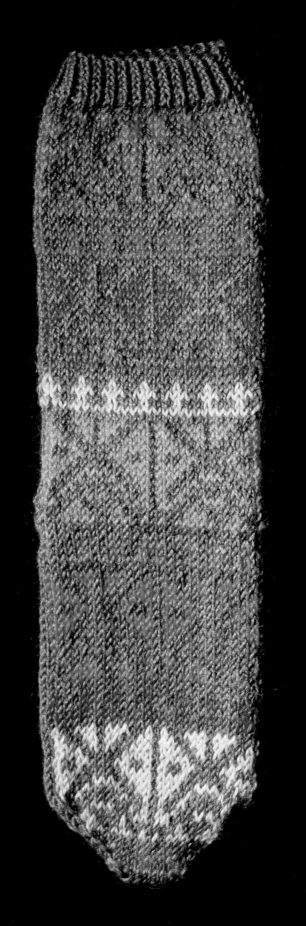

10

"Flag": 14 stitch, 14 row repeat
Secondary pattern: 4 stitch, 4 row repeat

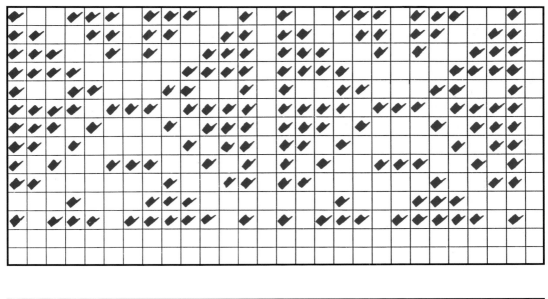

11

8 stitch, 10 row repeat

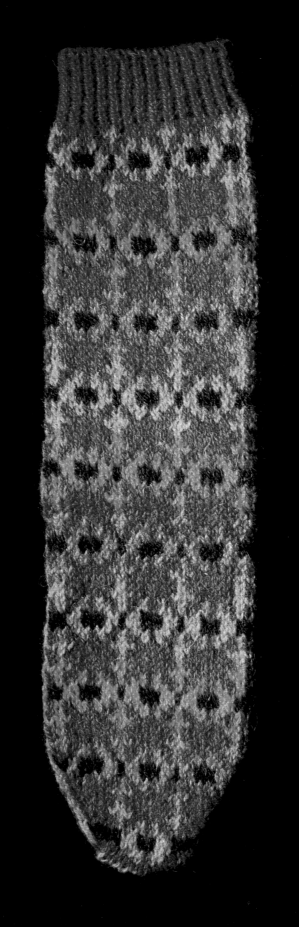

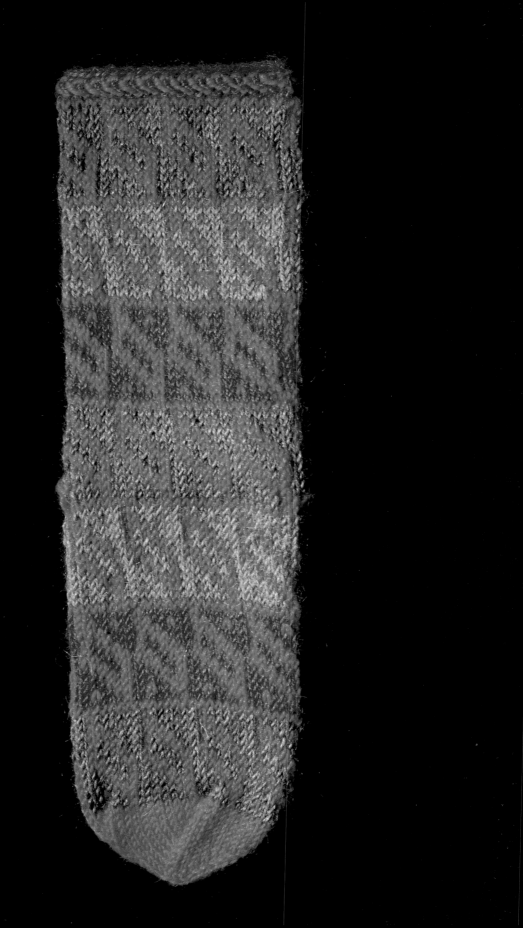

12

7 stitch, 12 row repeat

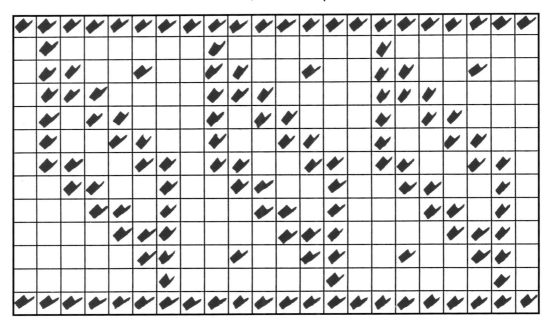

13

An authentic Turkish sock
"Wheel of Fortune"
16 stitch, 17 row repeat

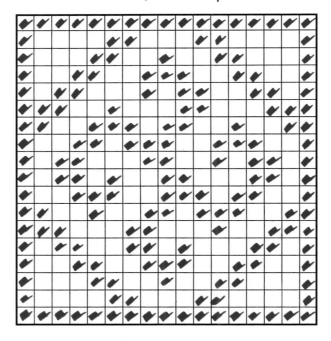

14

Wedding sock from the Black Sea region
Foot pattern: 41 stitch, 39 row repeat

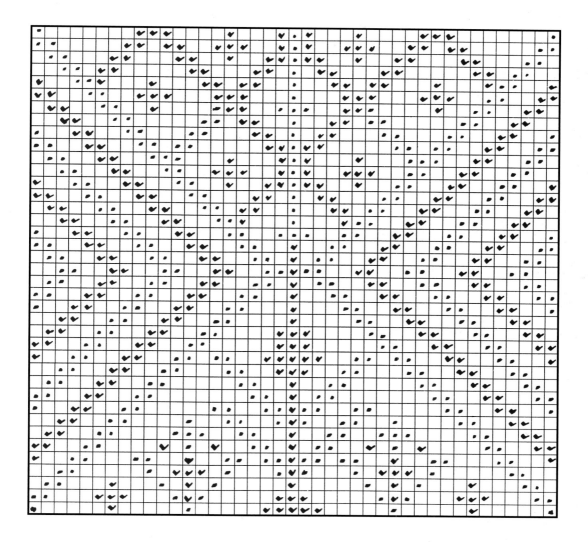

Leg patterns:
"Hook": 8 stitch, 11 row repeat
(without the third color, a very rhythmic pattern to knit)
Intermediate patterns: 3 stitch, 8 row repeat
(The third variation was caused by a mistake in the second row.)

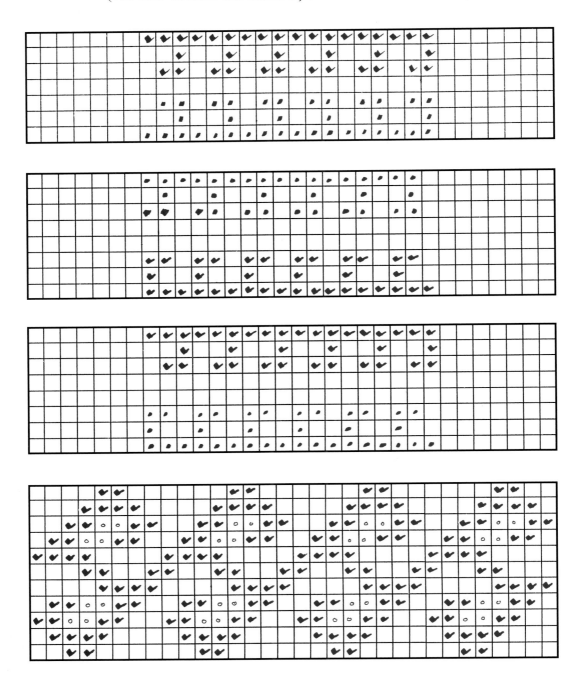

A woman's sweater knitted in the "well buckets" pattern.

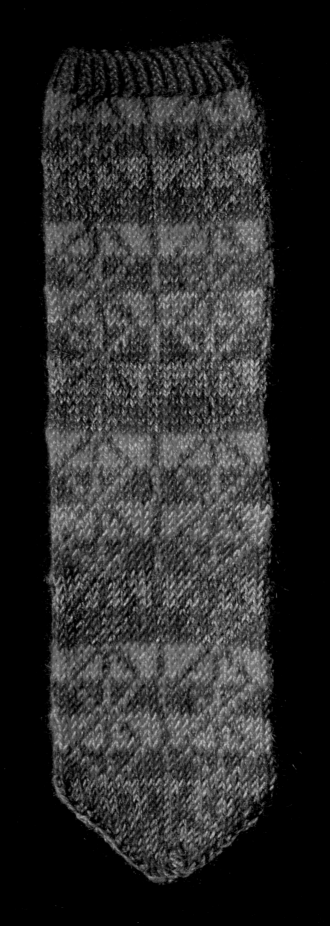

15

"Well Buckets"
14 stitch, 8 row repeat

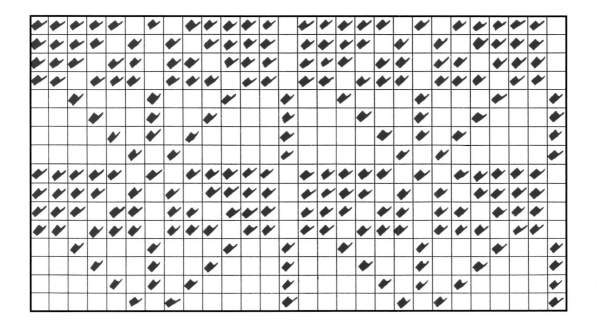

16

An authentic Turkish sock

Large pattern on foot: 41 stitch, 37 row repeat

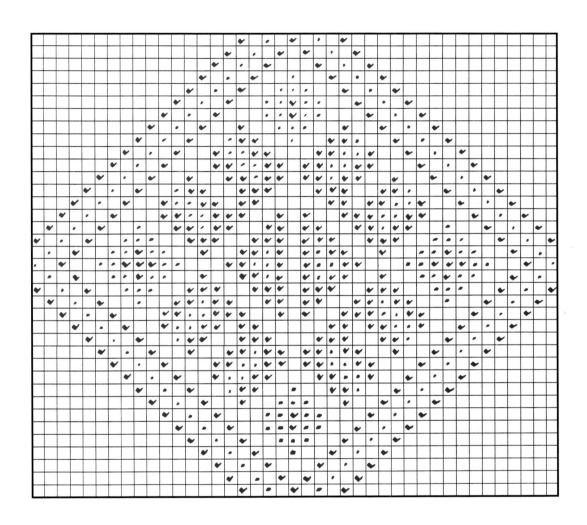

Small patterns on foot:
15 stitch, 7 row repeat
3 stitch, 5 row repeat
12 stitch, 14 row repeat

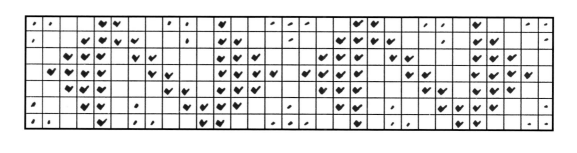

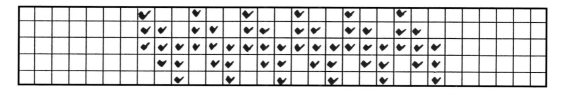

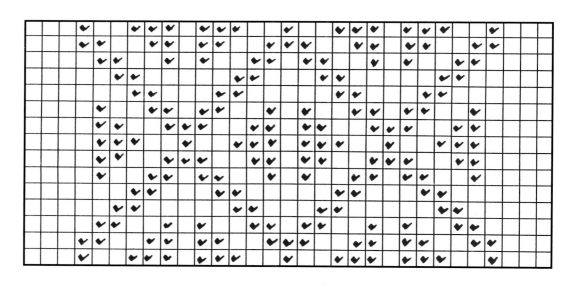

Leg pattern: 26 stitch, 30 row repeat

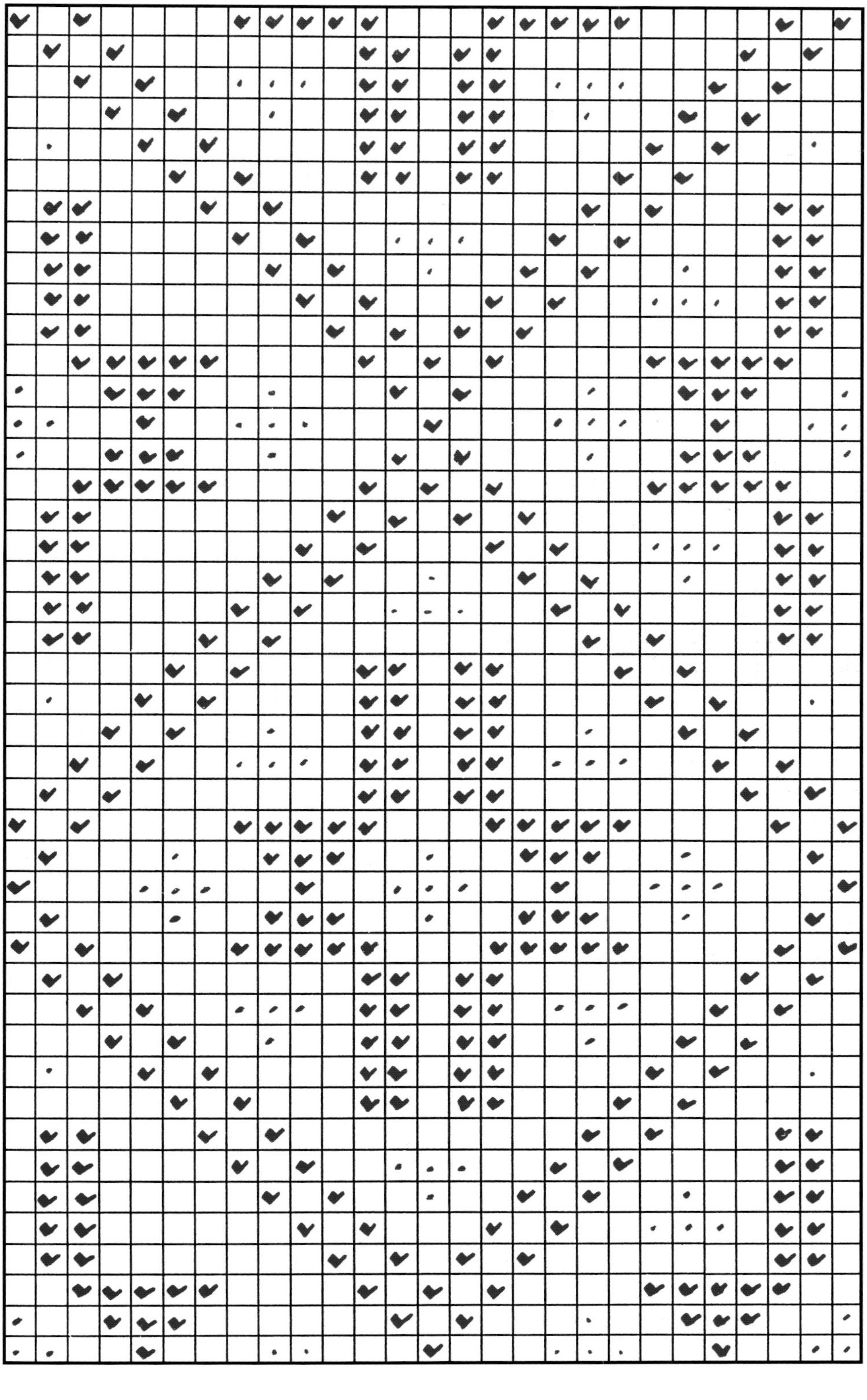

17

An authentic Turkish sock
"Heart Crook"
6 stitch, 10 row repeat
This pattern is derived from the lower portion of the common hook (see sock 31).

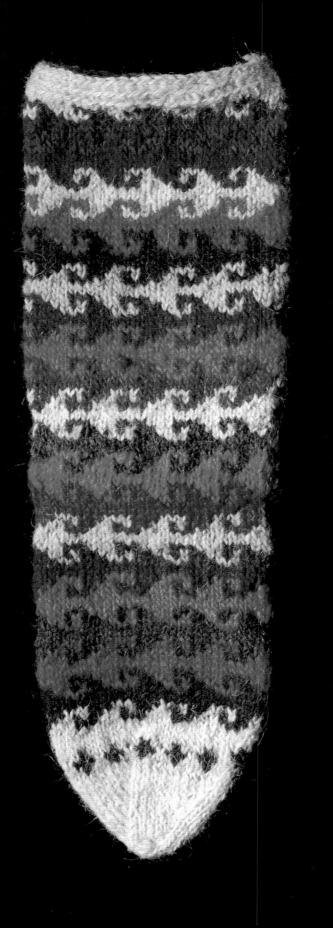

18

Authentic Kurdish sock from eastern Turkey
15 stitch repeat, reversed at center
15 row repeat

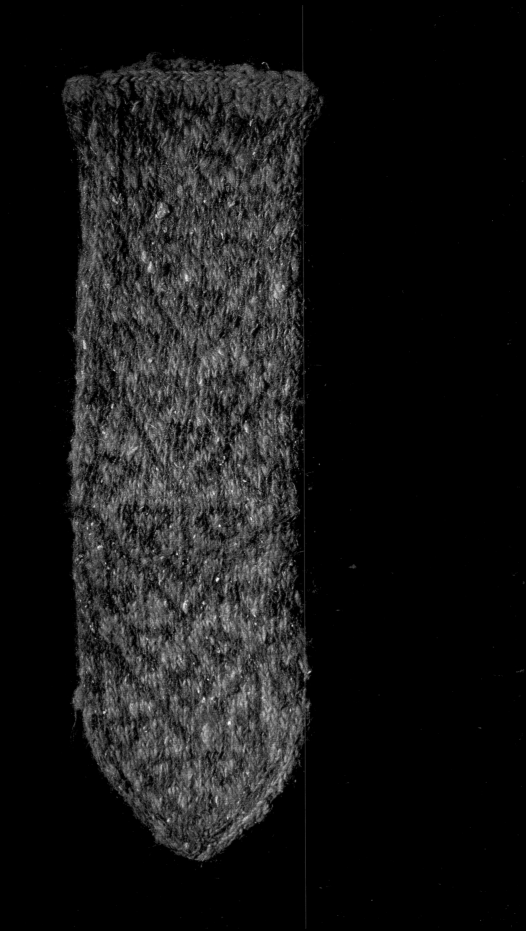

19

"Apple"

14 stitch, 14 row repeat

An authentic Turkish sock with a modern simplification of the common heart crook
"Triangles"
4 stitch, 10 row repeat

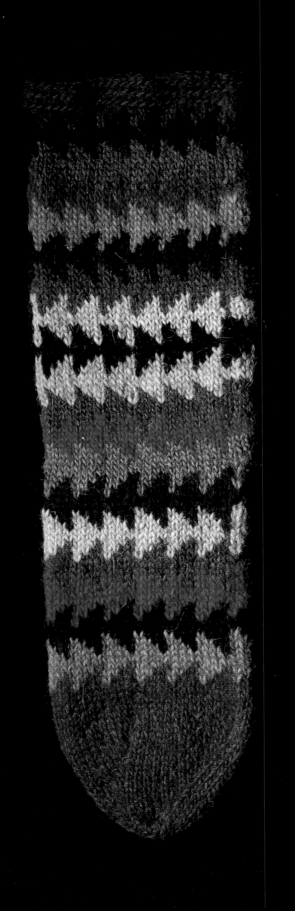

"Hook": 6 stitch, 7 row repeat
"Rose": 25 stitch, 8 row repeat
(This is a particularly pleasing pattern to knit)

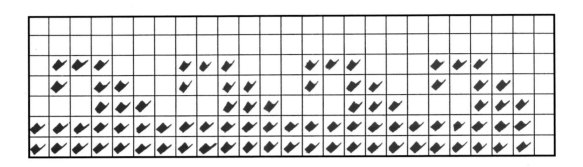

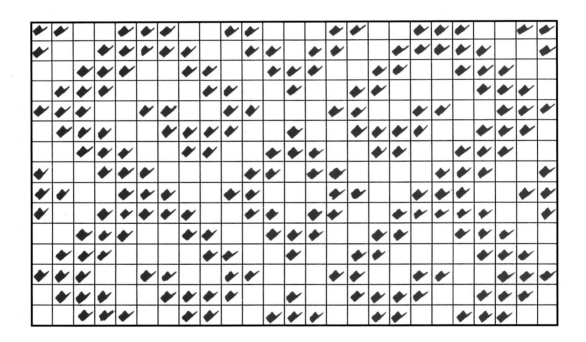

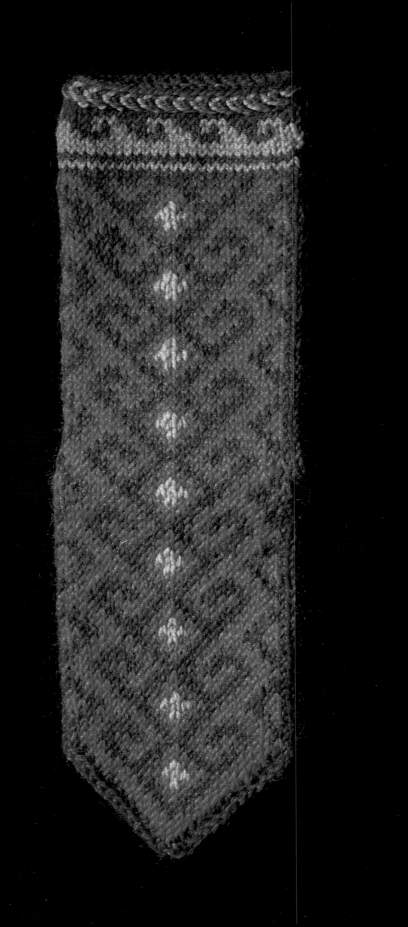

"Ivy"
12 stitch, 12 row repeat

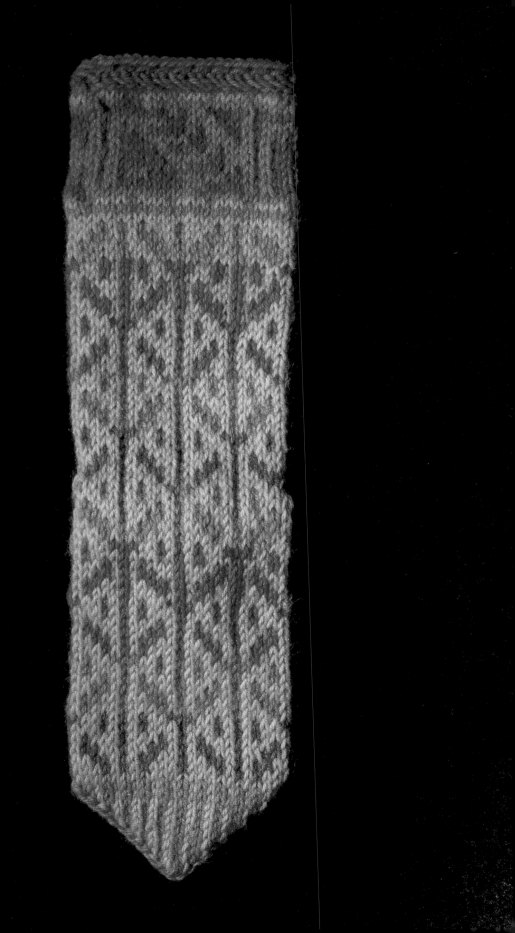

25 stitch, 28 row repeat

24
"Moth"
18 stitch, 10 row repeat

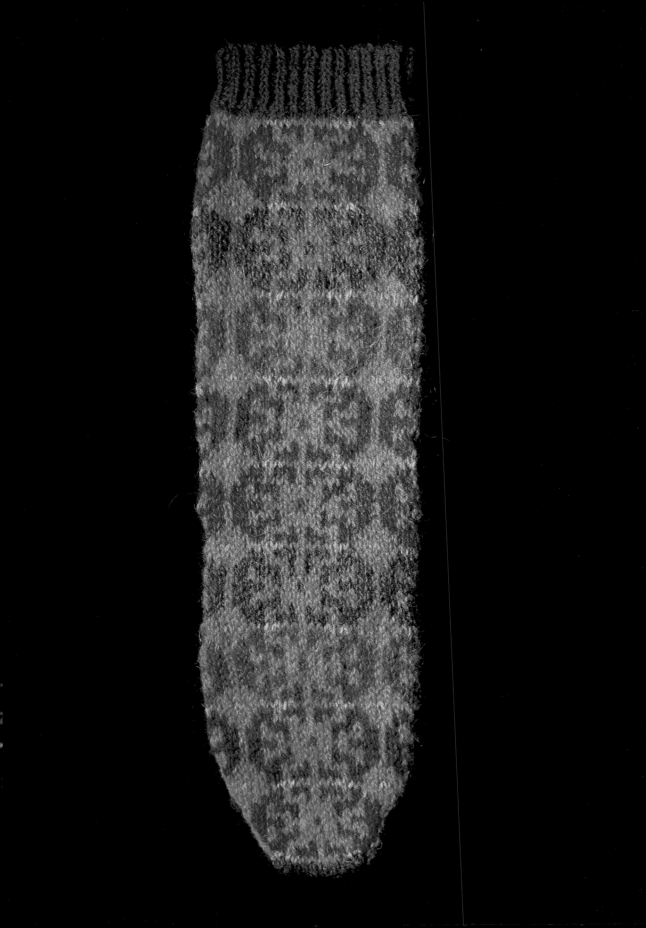

25

Secondary pattern at top: 2 stitch, 5 row repeat
"Burr": 8 stitch, 5 row repeat

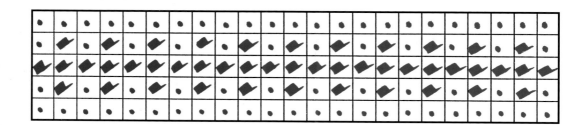

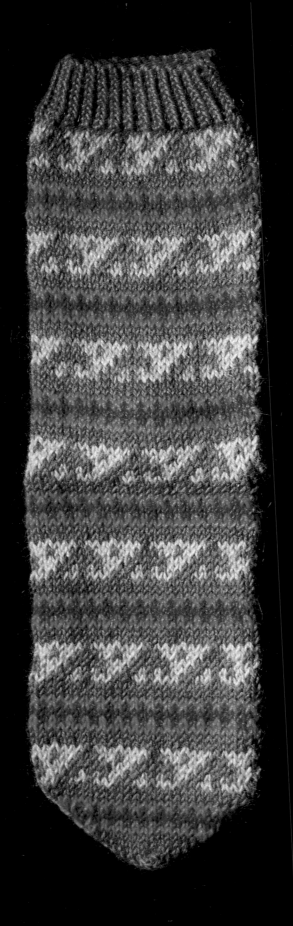

26

"Young Man's Moustache"
18 stitch, 16 row repeat

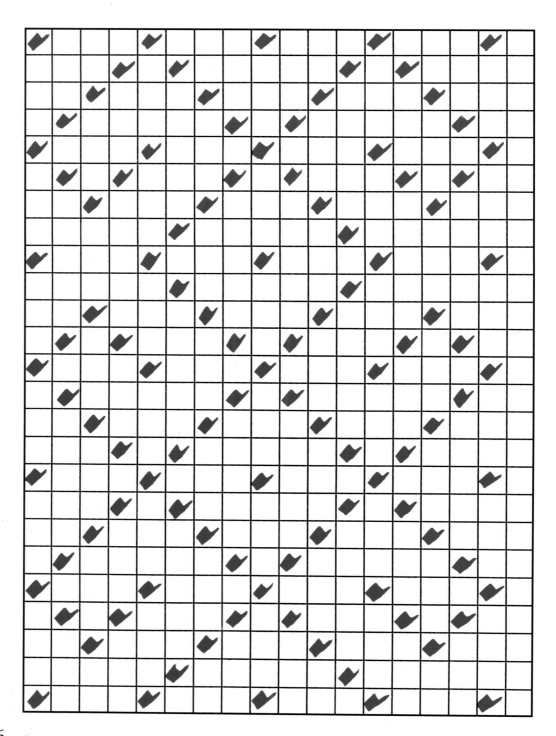

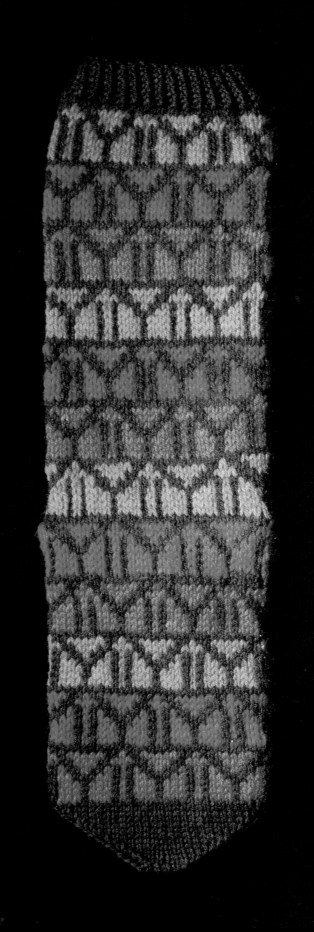

27

"Grub"

10 stitch, 8 row repeat

This vest is made
in the pattern
shown on
sock 23.

The front of this cardigan
is made in the
"Kurdish kilim" pattern.

A man's sweater
made in the
"crazy curl"
pattern.

Her sweater
is done in the
main pattern
shown
on sock 9.

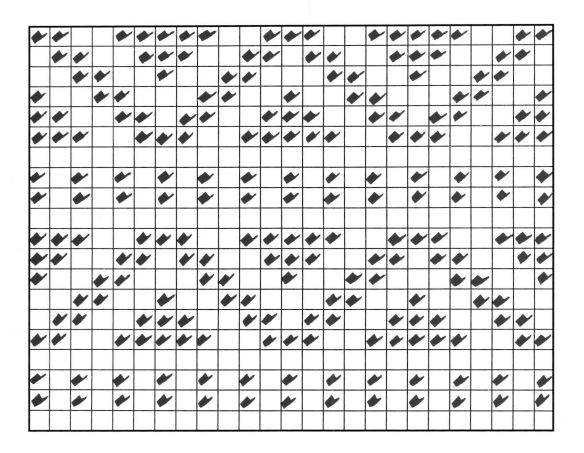

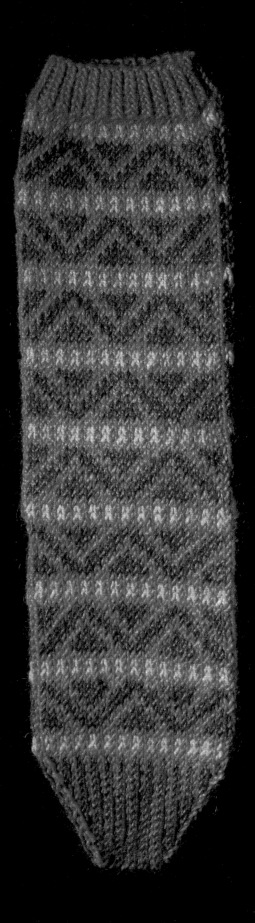

29

"Kurdish Kilim"

12 stitch repeat, reversed at center
12 row repeat
There are only two different pattern rows in this design.

30

"Head to Head": 11 stitch, 10 row repeat
"Sheep's Eye": 24 stitch, 13 row repeat for overall pattern

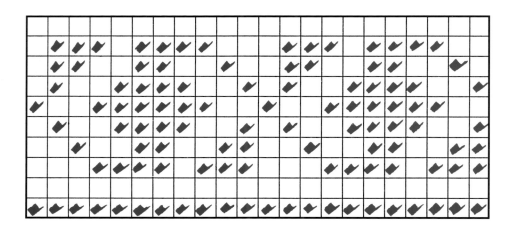

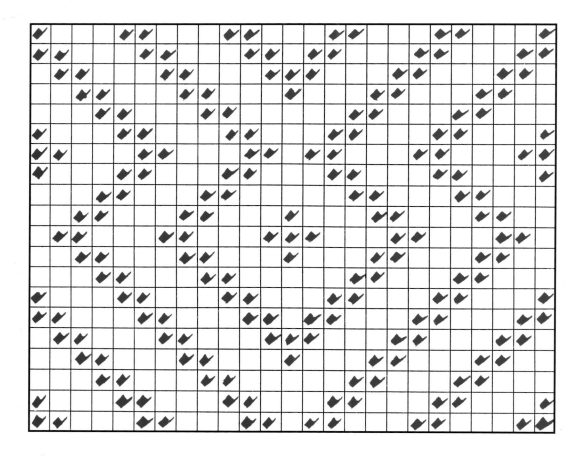

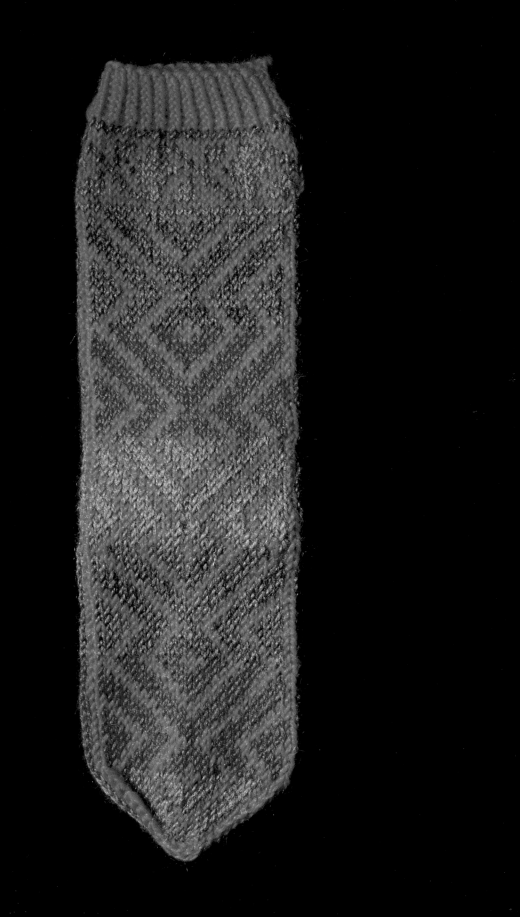

31

"Ram's Horn": 26 stitch, 26 row repeat
"Hook": 6 stitch, 7 row repeat

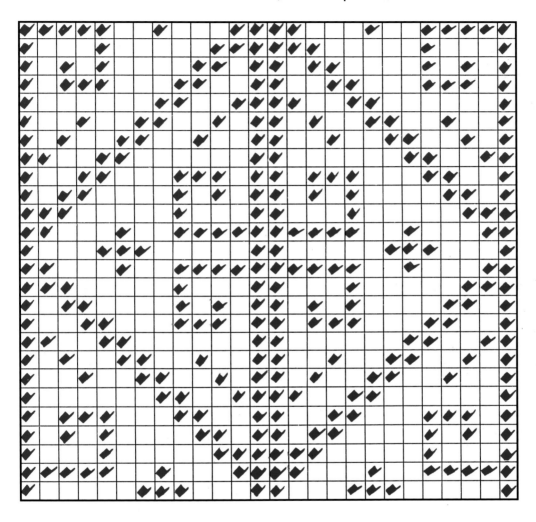

Secondary pattern at top: 12 stitch, 7 row repeat
"Boxes": 6 stitch, 10 row repeat

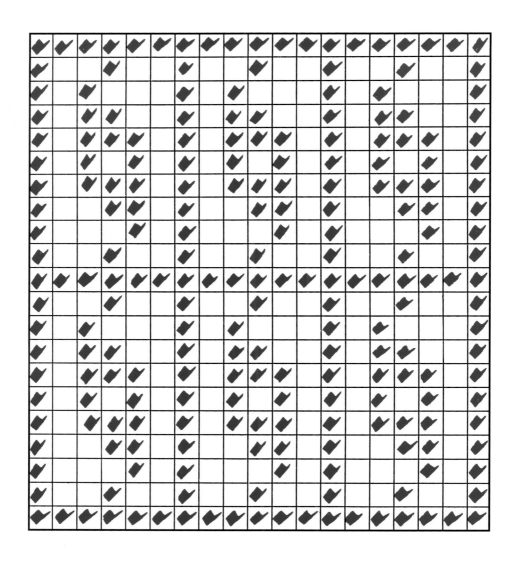

"Crazy Curl"
20 stitch, 14 row repeat

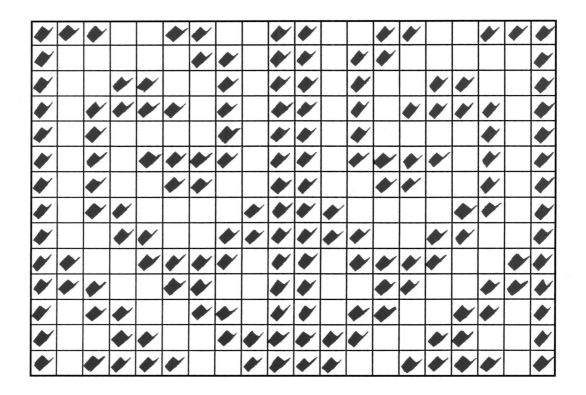

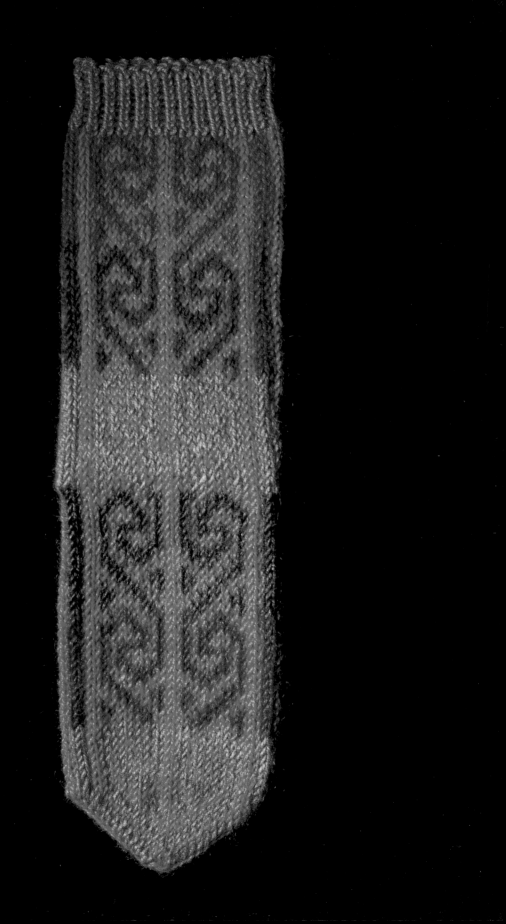

34

"Turcoman's Earring"
14 stitch, 22 row repeat

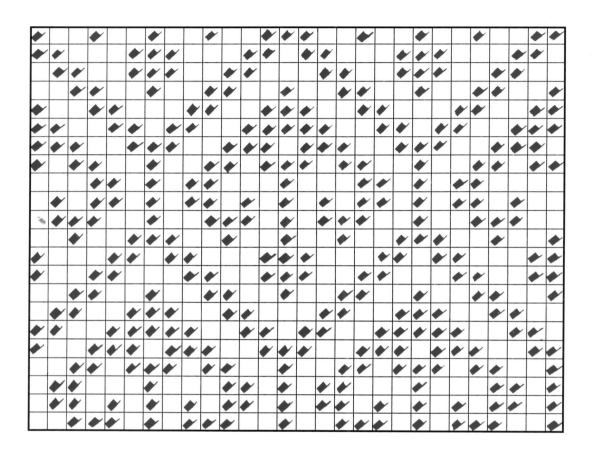

35

8 stitch, 14 row pattern

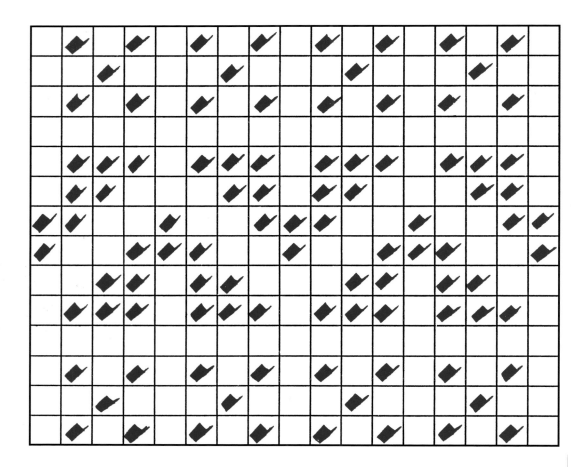

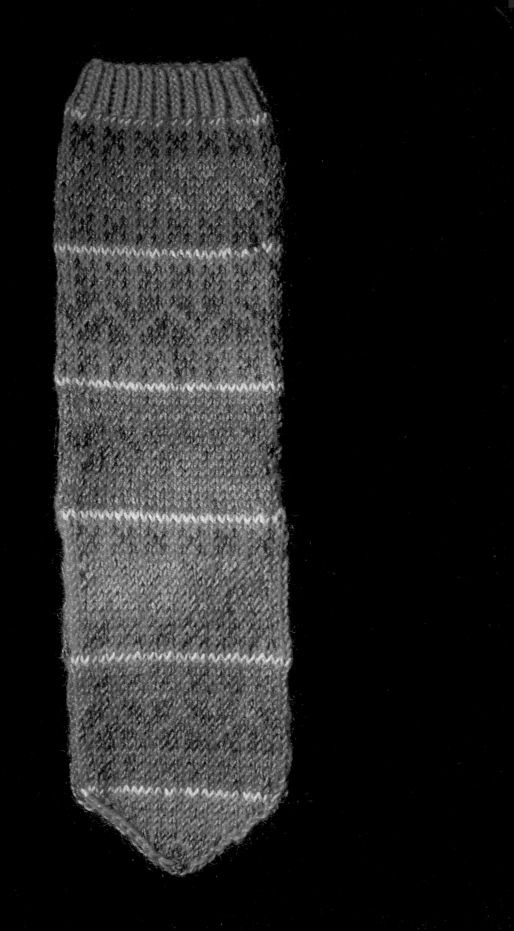

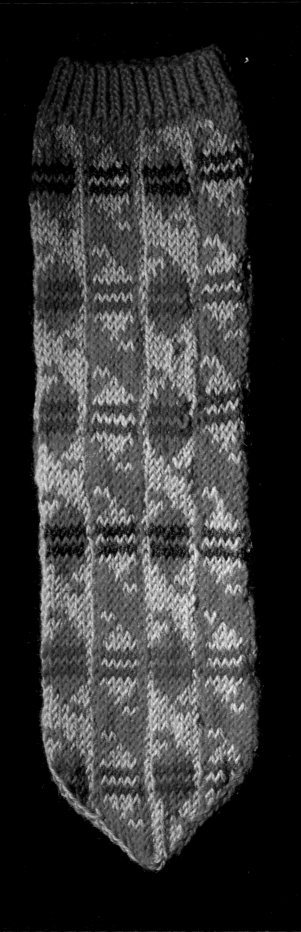

"Fez Tassel"
14 stitch, 14 row repeat

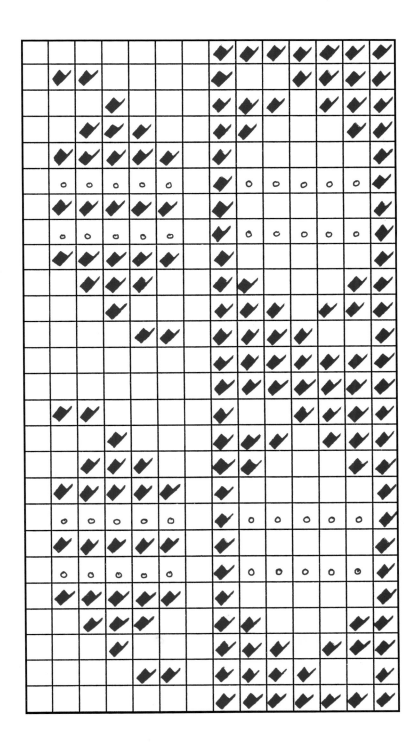

An authentic Turkish sock with old patterns, but knit from the top down—
a Western innovation. All of the small patterns are 5 rows, but they are 8,
6, and 9 stitch repeats, respectively. The foot pattern, an apple combined
with squares, is a 16 stitch, 18 row repeat.

100

38

Side strip: 5 stitch, 4 row repeat

"Ram's Horn": 18 stitch, 9 row repeat for overall pattern

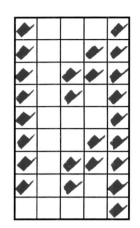

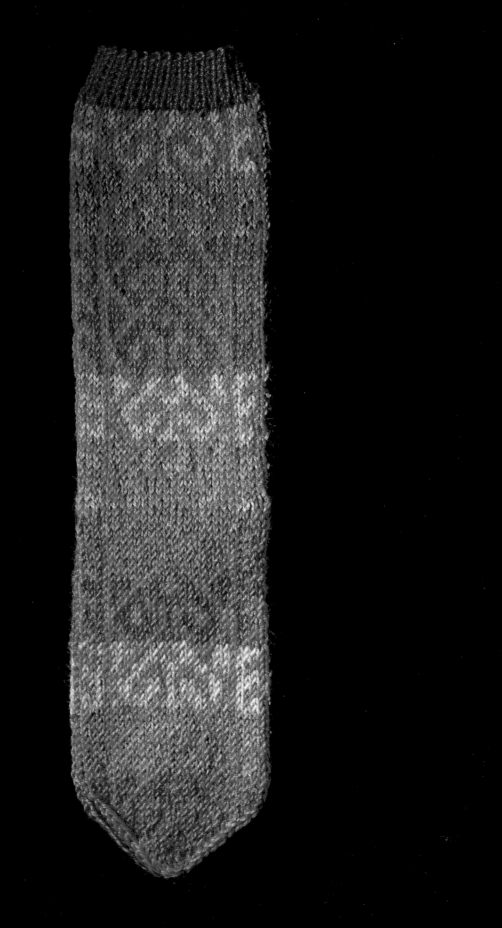

"Fez Tassel": 8 stitch, 9 row repeat
"Walnut Kernel": 8 stitch, 4 row repeat

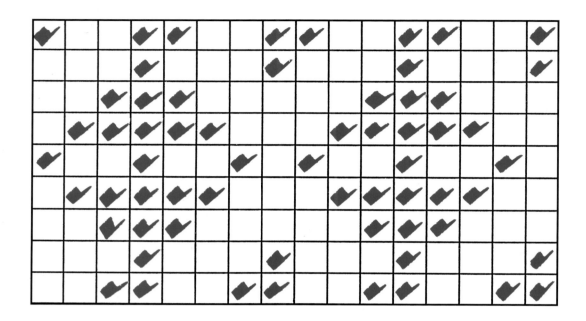

"Winged Gate of Paradise"
12 stitch, 17 row repeat

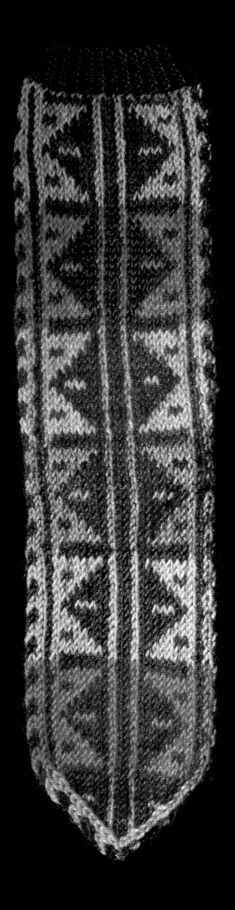

"Kilim Design"
22 stitch, 14 row repeat

"Willow Branch"
17 stitch, 7 row repeat

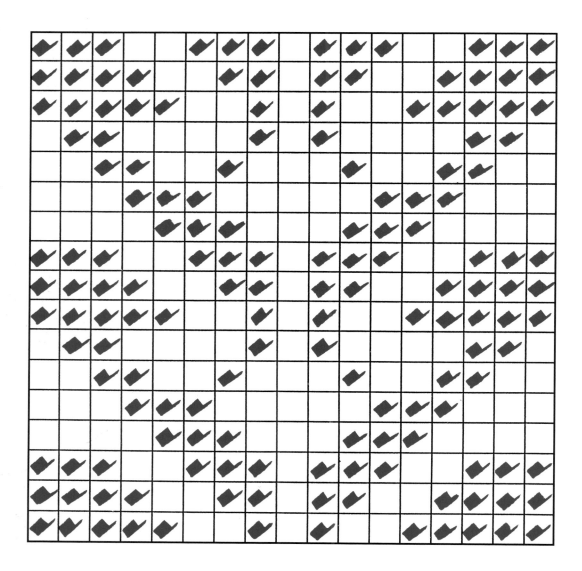

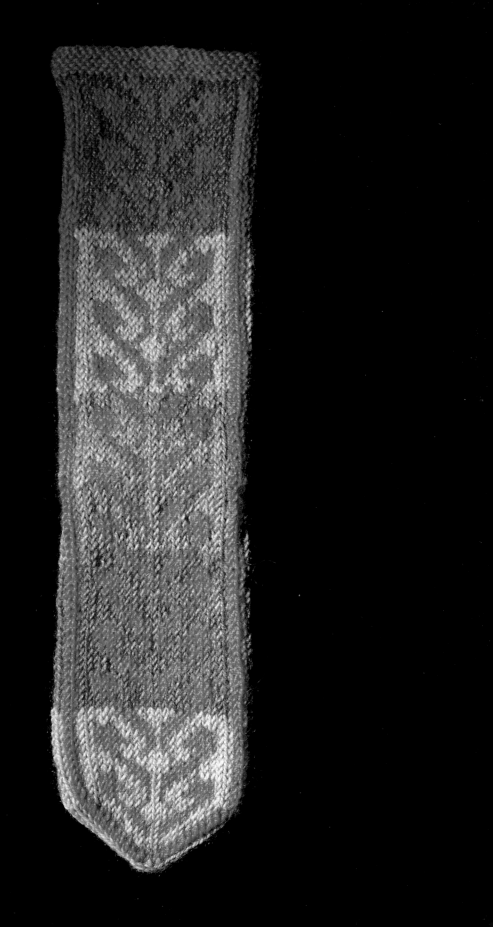

43

Foot pattern:
"Apple": 27 stitch, 35 row repeat

Leg patterns:
Intermediate pattern at top: 2 stitch, 5 row repeat
"Beetle": 14 stitch, 13 row repeat

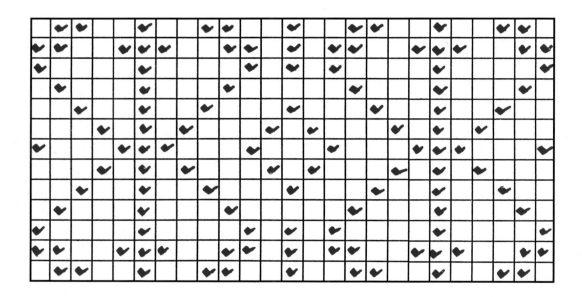

44

An authentic Turkish sock
Foot pattern:
"Apple": 40 stitch, 32 row repeat

Leg pattern: 40 stitch, 32 row repeat

45

"Crook": 10 stitch, 10 row repeat
"Decorations": 29 stitch, 29 row repeat

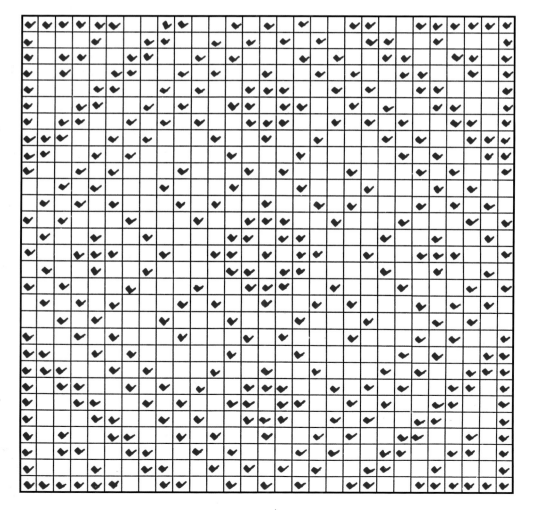

Sole Patterns

2 stitch, 2 row repeat

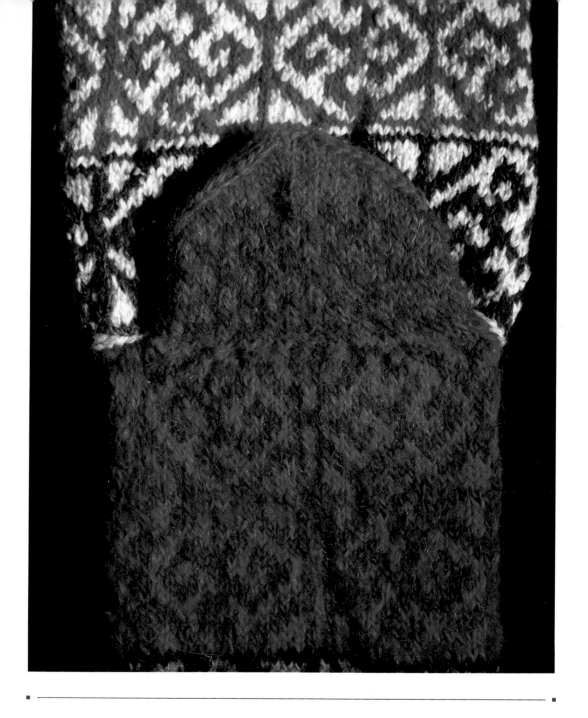

4 stitch, 4 row repeat

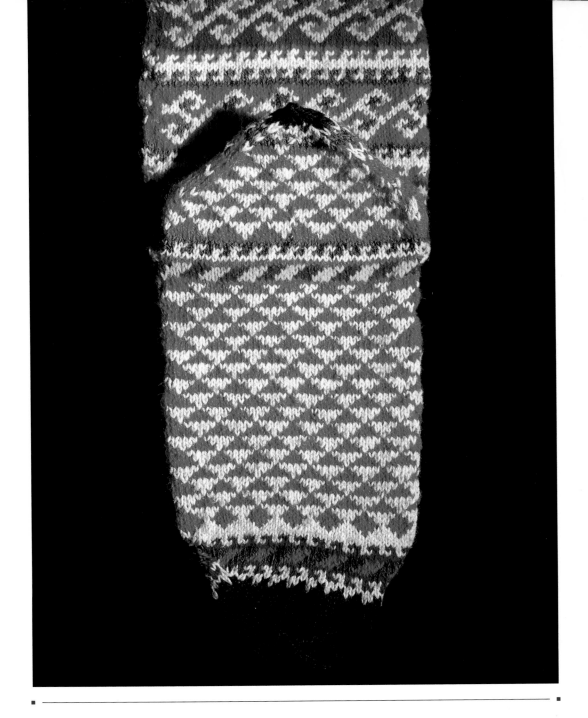

6 stitch, 6 row repeat

4 stitch, 4 row repeat

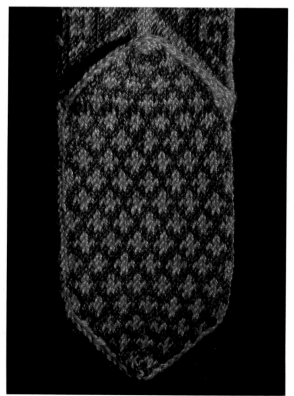

4 stitch, 6 row repeat

4 stitch, 8 row repeat

4 stitch, 4 row repeat, reversed at center

4 stitch, 2 row repeat

Index